As humans we experience growth in more than enough ways throughout our lives. Whether your religious beliefs affect you or your personal beliefs affect you, we must learn to grow and go on from the things that hurt us most. Below is an intriguing insight to what I have experienced in my short life thus far and what has gotten me through. With this combination of religion, advice, and personal stories, I hope to open doors for the minds of others and show them that pain is natural and growth will soon come; pain is only temporary.

With many thanks and love,

Morgan Mortimer

The Start of It All

In life we grow up in places that have everlasting impacts on us, not just us physically but emotionally as well. However, not all of those impacts are positive. The darkness can creep up on even the brightest souls and work its way into your life permanently. Keep your guard up and your faith even higher; remember, sometimes it takes more than just water to put out a fire.

I Was Raised Here

Living in the country is a beautiful thing
In the mornings dew covered everything and the
birds sang clear
I was raised here.

But the people, the people knew everything and
listened in on things they had no right to from
ear to ear
When someone chose to be different they were often
noted as "unclear" or "weird"
I was raised here.

Soon my growth was stunted and I fell into a path
of loneliness and fear
Trapped in my own mind, to others I really was
weird
But I was raised here.

Living in the country soon became more of an
unpleasant thing
And the dew that covered everything seemed to
literally consume Everything
Even the birdsong couldn't get me out of bed in
the morning
It seems that what I thought I knew really was
unclear
But I was raised here.

Fearfully Awake

I'm awake again
not because I can't sleep this time
But because of all the noise you're causing
downstairs

You're scaring us by the way you speak to her
except "She" is not just anyone
She just so happens to be our mother

Can't you see the pain you're causing her?
Isn't it clear by the way she shudders every time
you raise your voice?

Can you see the pain you're causing me?
Is this really how you think of me?
Your destructive expositions are replayed in my
head from day to day
I often wonder why she chooses to stay

This anger inside you tears our family apart from
each other
What is it going to take for you to not hurt me,
my siblings, or my mother?

His Calling to Me

Nourishment comes from many things
We need nourishment in order to survive and keep our minds
and bodies healthy

But the danger in this illness is that we see nothing that
fits
Not because we don't want to nourish ourselves, but because
we feel we don't deserve it

We feel unworthy and suffer from the most outrageous
thoughts… but they are our own
Soon, not only do our minds consume the nourishment we once
had but the mumbling from others takes the rest

What they see isn't what we see
What they feel isn't what we feel

I make dents in my own skin in order to feel the slightest
bit human
And you see that as weakness and look down on me for my
choices

Not long does this illness completely take away every ounce
of nourishment left
My body starts to show weakness,and my mind can no longer
keep up

Some of us get sent away
And others are forced by their own actions

But there are the lucky few that even after they thought
they had nothing left He appears
His scripture fills us with the nourishment we needed most
And soon our bodies and minds are transformed into something
healthier than before

That is what saved me
He saved me

I chose to turn my life around and walk down his path
And although I may still struggle with depression
The Lord has managed to continue to guide me in his
direction

Reminder:

At times the Lord's biggest blessings are our unanswered prayers. What I use to pray for, I now regret everyday. For I am now living in the moment of this wonderful life in every way. Unanswered prayers are the lessons, people, and the choices he didn't have to make for us because they didn't fit into the plan He had in store. His blessings can be the ones that leave us heartbroken and sore, for those are the blessings that teach us what we must steer away from evermore. Blessings come in forms of not just happiness but sadness as well. They show us that even though we may want something, it may not want us in return. Not everything in life will go your way. Give it up to God and learn to live yours day by day.

In Our Darkest Moments

Though the night may seem eerie to many
It spoke volumes to others

in a world where we become so reliant on People
The darkness makes us feel alone at times

This is why we are afraid of the dark
We are afraid of not having a sense of what is
coming or what lies right around the corner

So we stand put
We cling to the closest thing around us and we
don't let go til morning

But we're blind in the darkness
For fear is the devil working his way into our
souls

The Lord is always with us no matter light or dark
It is up to you if you choose to open up your
heart

A Pleasant Surrounding

These empty fields surrounding me seem to be the
only things that bring me happiness
I take a deep breath in
And let another deep breath out

It's moments like these that God reveals His true
beauty to us
There's nothing fake about nature
And there are no secrets to hide

It's time that I achieve some peace of mind

What You Did To Me:

Just when I thought no one could accept me
You found me

You took me places unimaginable
You showed me a side of myself I thought I had
lost forever

I grew close to you
Your scent and your smile
Even the way you got angry made me love you and
feel like this was worthwhile

But soon that would all be gone
Vanish like there was nothing ever there
And for years you continued to stretch my love as
far as it could go
And somehow you didn't seem to care

You used me
You blatantly and openly admitted to using me
You never loved me and took advantage of all the
love I had to give

Until one night you had enough courage to admit
What it seemed like you had been hiding all along
You played me in the end
Just like the lies you would tell yourself
Only believe you were doing no wrong

Now i'm the one hurting again
I'm back to my "normal" state
I now turn to a bottle
Just to forget my pain

A Mind Game

Even our closest enemies want to hear our deepest
secrets
So they can take the slightest bit of dignity we
have left
And use it against us

We become scared to open up
We become timid to let others know what we feel
And in return our minds become endless pits of
worry
Endless pits with a broken seal

Blind

Depression is being blind
Emotionless at times

Constantly being told how beautiful the world is
But simply not being able to find

Others describe to you the beauty they see
But for some reason you are not able to visualize

I often sit and ponder
When will I be able to see through mine

With Grandma

I ran up the hill everyday after school knowing
I'd get to see you
Walking in the front door and up that ramp
You were the first person I would cling to

You greeted me with warm coffee and cakes
Any mood I was in, you knew by my face

This soon became a normal routine growing up
Until one day they moved you and my whole world
changed up

I no longer had coffee with one of the women I
loved most
But every time I drank it I knew you were still
close

You may not be here in this small town
but never forget
You will always be my most cherished memory around

My Dear Friend

Growing up there weren't many people we could
relate to

We had found each other at a young age
It appeared we needed to

For living in this small town had little perks
But our friendship has managed to last through all
of the ups and downs life threw at us

And as we stand here today, a few years older
I'm not sure where my life would have been
If you had not given me your friendship or your
shoulder

The Ruin

What leads us to think these demeaning thoughts
about ourselves?
No matter how well I may do something
I can never fully accept the truth of doing
something well

Darkness seems to cover any positive thing in my
life
Never feeling good enough, I feel inclined to hide

Perhaps happiness was never meant for me
Perhaps I don't deserve anything good this world
has to offer
Maybe if I shut myself out long enough
People will forget about me and they will continue
to prosper

Reminder:

Far too often we are both the authors and victims of our own trauma. This trauma can be either mental or physical, but for some of us it is both. If you have found yourself stuck in a cycle where you constantly get up but can't seem to stand up fully, you may have found yourself trapped in a whirlwind of depression, fear, or anxiety. Don't be afraid. Learn to take your demons and do with them what you can. Through your struggle you will find growth and develop in ways beyond your belief. Your illness doesn't define you and you should never allow it. Many days are going to seem rough but you can and you will pull through regardless. Learn to embrace your pain, trials, and tribulations in order to reach new heights and places. The reward will truly be priceless and soon your once-empty soul will be one that cannot be shattered into pieces.

The Mind

I can feel myself drawing closer and closer to my
own end
Drowning in a pool of lies and inner thoughts
For this I cannot stand

My heart aches for acceptance
But my mind reassures me that will never come

For it is hard when you are trapped within your
own mind
To easily run and escape from

Judge Me

They judge me
I know they do
Why must they act like we live in a perfect world
That can only be filled with a perfect few?

And how can you sleep at night
Knowing you're just like everyone else
Not allowing others around you to be different
All because you are not content with yourself

Tough

Every scar on my body reminded me of the blood I had drawn

My skin often ached at the slightest touch
But the impressions and indentations left behind showed that I was strong enough

Wanting to change everything about yourself wears down both your mind and your body
But you are tough.

Continue battling your demons and see things become new
Do everything you can to become the best version of a better **you**

Broken

I can't stop these thoughts from coming back

It feels like shards from broken glass have
pierced into different sections of my body
Although nothing is actually there

I'm ripping my own heart in half
By lowering my own personal standards
And never looking back

Unsure of what may fix me
Or what my future may hold
I continue to deteriorate on the inside
With my skin showing all of the cracks

Trapped

How might someone open up their mind
When they have been trapped in their own for so
long

Pain and disappointment become normal to us
Feelings we can never truly erase

We try to find our way out
But instead we find ourselves getting more lost in
this place

Forcing Pain

Too often we complain about our feelings
We wish the pain and heartbreak would just go away
We wish our feelings were mute to almost anything

But when you have been numb for so long
To any sort of feeling or emotion that you must
hurt yourself in order to feel something again

You begin to wish all the pain and heartbreak
returned
For I would rather feel sadness, pain, and
happiness
Than feel forced to cause my own in order to be
heard

Reminder:

Who are we really? Do we ever actually figure that out? I find myself asking this question a lot lately. More so because I haven't found myself yet but then again I'm not sure if we ever fully do. Time and time again we question ourselves, our character, and our choices, as if we have to be found in a certain amount of time. Many of us are stuck in a world where there was never something okay with being who we are; we just don't know how to change that mindset permanently. The world surrounding us is changing just as much as we are, and it's okay to not know everything about ourselves just yet. What's the rush? Who says we can't figure ourselves out a few years down the road and learn from our own and others' lessons. Live for now and find peace in all of life's directions.

When someone asks you what depression feels like
It's almost too hard to describe

It feels like i'm stuck
Stuck sinking into a hole of nothingness
Stuck in a pit drowning in my own thoughts
throughout the day
Stuck in a maze surrounded by terrifying displays
and voices

My favorite colors are those of a darker spectrum
But it never used to be
Oh how I wish I could return to better ways
If I could only return to the old me

To Let Go

Its gloomy here
Always dull
Surrounded by feelings typically happy people are
scared of
But these I've learned to accept as a whole

Depression follows me wherever I go
It soon became the greatest friend that I knew
But sometimes our greatest friends are not our
healthiest
And this goes to show
That sometimes even our biggest problems
Are the hardest ones to let go

Voices

The voices in my head that I keep hearing will not
leave me be
Im searching frantically for something to break
the noise
But these demeaning thoughts wreak havoc and
hinder me

Why am I like this
Why can't I find joy in the silence
Why can't I just be happy with who I am
Instead of resorting to personal violence

The positive and negative in me keep clashing
like a war is starting within me
While the outside of me is slowly collapsing

Please make these thoughts go away
I'm not sure how I'm going to live the rest of my
life
If I can't learn to get rid of this pain

To Know We Are Alive

I'm not sure if i'm getting better
Or just getting better at hiding it

It's a funny thing that some of us bleed
Just to know that we are still alive
There's no denying this

Heal Over

Perhaps it is meant for the broken
To use our bodies as a canvas
With the intentions of recovery
Our bodies show our weaknesses

But along with recovery
The scars will still linger
Using what is left behind as an example
To show that even the worst damages will heal over

The Corner

The far corner in my room is where I find myself
every so often
I stare into nothing
As if something will appear

The thoughts of agony and hateful words seem to be
all I can hear
And soon my skin becomes the place it mainly shows
Trying to hide the scars
But most people should know

That scars run much deeper than the skin
This I can confirm
Although I don't pierce my own skin anymore
It's my inner thoughts that continue to cause this
hurt

A Test to My Sanity

As time grew on, my life in this small town seemed to nearly rip apart every ounce of happiness I had left. Being strong is tough. Our whole lives we are told to move on or just "get over it," but some things we never do. At times we are put into situations where we feel so low but we must act so strong. And for what? For now, we need to learn how to live a little so it is possible for love and happiness to find us despite what we may have been through. Everyone hits their own weak points at a certain age or time. Remember that no flower blossoms at the same time as any other buds on the tree. Soon it will be both yours and mine, and oh how exciting that will be.

As I Look out this packed car window
Every problem I had here begins to seem so little

For I was going off and finally leaving
I think I am ready for what could be my new
beginning

A Time To Blossom

We all blossom at different times
I wonder when it will be mine
I'll sit and be patient
And I'll Act on his time
For I know what he wants
May not be what I have in mind

In Front of You

We are a product of our own experience
That is safe to say

But what is here today may not be a different day
Make the most of everything
Including what you have

For our experiences shape us, Yes
But our loved ones make up the other half

Oftentimes we take some of the people we love and care for
most for granted. This poem is dedicated to Tyler
Cherrington, Ramsey Adams, and TC Loyd as their lives were
taken from them far too early in 2017/2018. Hold those you
love most close to your heart and don't be afraid to
document the memories you make. Life flashes quite often
before our eyes. What a shame it is that some of us aren't
lucky enough to see another day.

They Always Leave

You were the background noise of my life
Making yourself prominent when no one else would
Making me believe in good people again
Making me feel understood

Soon that was taken away abruptly
You completely disappeared
My trust was misused again
My heart continued to tear

When will someone come along and make me feel
whole?
When will gray skies and dimly lit rooms quit
making me feel comfortable?

Falling deeper and deeper into my own sadness
Parts of me that were once put together are no
longer whole

Lies Within You

And every little piece of your heart I wanted
All of the happiness you once shared with me, I
wanted to share with the world

For you opened up my eyes to much more than love
And showed me I was different than just any girl

You opened my heart up to new beginnings
And somehow closed doors on things I needed to end

But once you got up and left
I knew my heart was in need of more than a friend

How could someone that brought me so much joy keep
all of these secrets untold
Do you not think someone like you is capable of
feeling whole?

Our True Condition

To love ourselves we must grasp the version God
knit together
Trust that our insecurities make us stronger
And believe that we are precious in God's sight

When we are granted peace by Him
We are also given peace that's everlasting
Calming all of our fears, easing all our fright

As we mourn over our true condition we are brought
to a realization
And this is what will lead us to change

For the pain God wants us to experience
Is the pain that allows us to rely on His Grace

Emotion

We feel worthless at times
There's no describing why

People tell you that you're worth so much more
But when someone doesn't treat you that way
Your heart ends up feeling torn

We try to move on
Head in different directions

But our emotions get the best of us
Regardless of our intentions

A Hidden Attacker

In a world full of beauty
There is still a darkness that lurks
It creeps up behind you
It scares you with a smirk

Your soul is left feeling mangled
While your heart tries to fight back

Do not give into the devil's will
For he is used to being the one to attack

The Hurt I Cause

I hurt them
And by them I mean those I love most

I don't hurt them physically
But instead it's mental

For what they feel they have done for me isn't
enough
And being unable to control my emotions
Is something they can't continue to handle

More News

As soon as I thought things were going well
Bad news struck again
Our hearts can only be broken so many times
Until we feel them caving in

There are happy people and there are the unhappy
ones
Those who cover their sorrows show signs of fresh
tears impressed upon their cheeks
As people begin to look for answers their
mentality only begins to grow more weak

What will save our unhappy souls?
And why can it not be as simple as good food or
good company
The pain and sorrow will quickly return
Only to bring another day of dread and defeat

The Routine

It's not always the person we miss
Many times it's just the routine

We must learn to get over it
And focus on who we were meant to be

In your head

Why do you feel so inadequate
Is it something someone said?

If so, why are you allowing it to get to your
head?
If not, then what is causing all of this pain and
dread?

There is beauty in all of us
Then again some can't see
Allow yourself to fall in love
With the world, you, and Me

When I Talk About You

Sometimes I talk to God about you
I feel at ease when I do

But then an interrupting force bestows itself upon
me
And I realize that the devil is listening too

You have presented yourself to me in both your
purest and darkest forms
Therefore I know they are both listening
Because you are becoming deformed

How to be Loved

Remember that you are <u>not</u> meant to be loved in parts
But you are meant to be loved as a <u>whole</u> part

Therefore, if anyone only loves a part of you
They must only love a part of themselves in return

Sometimes it's hard realizing this
Your importance and your worth
When you have put yourself out there and gotten
nothing but hurt

Remember to rejoice in the simple things
You are more than capable of being accepted

Once you obtain a new mindset
There is no one that can wreck it

Progression

Many sad nights will creep on you from time to
time
No matter how wrecked you may think you are
Just remember you're still fine

Not all of your progress is gone because of one
bad day
Keep in mind that even a little positivity goes a
very long way

The Ways

Suppressed fears
And never-ending tears

Nothing can erase my past
This is clear

But there is always hope
There will always be better days

And although you may not be able to forget
You will begin to erase

Just what you thought you would have never
forgotten
By simply living through His ways

Within You

I found a calmness within you
The type of energy I felt no longer existed

Filled with happiness and grief
My whole heart felt twisted

Constantly being pulled in the right and wrong
directions
I fell in utter disbelief

How could someone like me be able to feel
something so pure?
For once I was beginning to feel complete

How We End

What causes us to walk past those who treat us
best?
When they have been the ones to accept us for the
way we are or dress

Perhaps we don't mean to push them away
But instead let our emotions determine who we see
compatible

You don't think you're good enough for even a
simple friend
So you shove everyone out
With no hesitation or question
Only to be left alone with just you and your
depression

Jumping into Pain

We must jump into pain in order to experience
life, glory, and love

Dwell in your own heart and others
And rest your worries on the man above

Love is easy
Don't make it hard
Let the peace of **God**
Guard your heart

Friends of Mine

Why are we so willing to give so much of ourselves
to others?
Is it because we receive no recognition for the
love we have to offer?

My heart is always being used, but I don't seem to
mind
Both loneliness and emptiness have become very
close friends of mine

Reminder:

Stop telling yourself that because you aren't happy with who you are or what you look like that you don't deserve love or even anything in general. Stop planting the idea in your head and others heads that if you don't love yourself then you are incapable of loving anyone or anything else in return. You are allowed to feel unhappy just as much as you are allowed to feel excited. What makes you think that you don't deserve to be loved when <u>our Creator</u> loves you endlessly and in fact is the true meaning of Love? There will always be someone there to love you even if you can't love yourself. That is the beauty in finding love or being the definition of love for someone else. That is the beauty in growth and having feelings. I promise a family member loves you, your pet loves you, or maybe even the stranger you met 10 minutes ago fell in love with something about you. The possibilities are endless. Fall in love with items, ideas, books, nature, God, etc. and go with it. Accept the fact that <u>you are capable</u> of loving all things and <u>then</u> choose to work on it towards yourself if you have to. We have time for anything we make time for. There are many problems and stressors in this world; don't fluster over the fact that nothing is going right for you at the moment. Most importantly, never sell yourself short of anything because you don't see fit. Find joy in the littlest of things and watch <u>nothing</u> phase you one bit.

When It Rains

Many times you won't understand it
You won't understand why when it rains it really
does pour
You won't understand how someone you gave your all
too
Left you in the dark with your heart on the floor

I will never understand it myself
And neither will you

But believe me when I say
There's something much bigger planned that's
coming soon

Another Day

Being alone is a terrifying feeling
I often rely on the stars and music to take me
away

The thoughts keep returning
Just when I think I'm over this pain

I realize it's not that easy to shake away
The stars and music will have to do for now
Getting better will happen another day

Alone

It's overwhelming
All of these new thoughts, friends, and places
I've experienced

I look at how much I've grown
And how much more confident I'm beginning to feel

The scary thing is
I refuse to think that this is real

I'm waiting for something detrimental to happen
But with all the people that have learned to rely
on me
I realize I possess this kind of emotional appeal

Even though I can't always help myself with my own
pain
That doesn't mean I can't help others with their
own
Sadly, we all have one thing in common
And that is the constant feeling of being alone

Strung Out

I can't seem to find an escape
How many of these chances I've taken over and over
Yet I can't get away from being the one that's
pushed over

I've given too many pieces of myself out to others
And some not enough

Talking about my past seems to scare too many of
you
So you leave me and turn the other way
While I struggle to get up

It's times like this that I need saved
I'm torn between what I must do
For someone to accept me and look beyond all of my
pain
Just so I can fall in love with myself and you

Anything But My Heart

You're making it hard for me
To even look your way

How is it that you out of all people feel okay
with hurting me?
It can't be possible you are unaware of what
you've done

I scream and cry and fall to my knees in the
privacy of my room
For weeks on end you have me second guessing what
I did to you

But I did nothing except let you in too far
I should have known that you may have wanted me
for other reasons
But you did not want my heart

What My Mind Is Telling Me

You think only those who care about you can hear
you when you're quiet

But I am always listening

They assure you that you weren't built to break
yet here you are in pieces

I am the voice you hear

Staying awake at night is your new routine because
sleep requires peace

You're welcome dear

When will I wake up from this nightmare?
When will someone shake this out of me?
I can't take this voice much longer
It is my biggest enemy

Drifting

We are drifters
Those with no set path or guidance

Not sure what lies ahead
But certain that <u>He</u> will guide us

For Those Who Struggle

Hold on
Please, I'm begging you
Hold on to these emotions and people
And learn to never let go

Life will get rough but never slow down
Drown yourself in love and laughter
Instead of chasing it down

Hold onto your knowledge of life
And the lessons you have learned
Forcing pain or drinking it away
Does nothing but leave you more damaged in return

What You Were To Me

You were the sound of melodies
Mixed with the fresh smell of roses
Two things I could never grow tired of
No matter how much I was around it

The simplicity of you embraced me in such a way
That even my worst days could be fixed
But the moment you started distancing yourself
I knew those smells and melodies were going to be
truly missed

Reminder:

We all need someone to love and trust. But it appears as though some of us don't even trust ourselves enough. We are often too good at running away, and in return we force those we love and care for to sit on the sidelines and watch us struggle. Rejecting any hint of confrontation that we need to seek help. When I'm not trapped in the midst of my own mind, I can be found behind a smile. I try to help others around me in order to feel alive the slightest bit, but that high can only last for so long. Thankfully to the man above, I have never felt more at peace with my lifestyle. If there is one thing I can ask of you, let it be this: quit rejecting the love and help others stretch out to you. Quit rejecting God's plan for you and convincing yourself there is no hope or purpose for your life at this time. Seek Him with all of your heart and allow his light to guide your ways. We prove ourselves by our purity, understanding, patience, and sincere love. The difficulties presented into our lives are meant to help us grow spiritually. This way we may be able to live by faith instead of just feeling.

Here's To Hoping

Reassurance is something we as people tend to look for. Our reasons for seeking reassurance may be based off our experiences throughout our lives or may be based off the simple fact that it feels good to feel accepted. Whatever your reasoning may be, remember to never lose sight of your dreams. Stay excited about them. Stay excited about new challenges, people, and experiences that you will encounter all throughout your life. Who is going to stop you from doing something other than yourself? Our Saviour is going to be with you every step of the way and will guide you to everlasting happiness and health. Here's to hoping my friends. Here's to hoping and working toward better days and bettering ourselves both internally and externally. In doing so you will not only help others around you, but most importantly you will also help yourself. My biggest hope for you is that when someone tells you to live life to the fullest you don't just take that and run with it, but instead you go out and do it. Do what makes you feel good and watch things fall in place. We can only receive as much as we put in, and for this we have faith.

<u>My Promise</u>

The human experience shouldn't be kept inside
For what we experience in our lives is what shapes
us
Be proud of who you are and the work you've
accomplished
Even the little things you do in life will take
you far
I promise.

What Is Yours

There's always time to change
And if it's not time that changes you
Then maybe it is someone who will change you

Someone willing to grow and change with you
Maybe that someone just happens to be yourself
No matter the circumstance
It always begins with what you want to change or
maybe who you want to change for

The world is yours my friends
Go and explore

What Lies Beneath

Once you've hit rock bottom
I hope you realize that you have

I hope you begin to escape and make your way back
up
It's a sick thing to believe you are stuck

There is always a way
At times we lose sight of it, yes
But it is never too far
It's never too late to free yourself from all of
the pain trapped behind those scars

A Prayer

Far too often do we forget about Him and who He is
Luckily, he is generous enough to always forgive

What a wonderful feeling
The peace that He brings
The good feelings inside that take us to our knees

Thank you heavenly Father
For always reminding us just how precious this
life is

Reminder:

Believe it or not, happiness is a choice. It's choosing to surround yourself with those who allow you to feel comfort within yourself on the days you don't. You will eventually realize who matters, who never did. We often hate hearing the phrases "you will get over it" or "just give it time," but it is true. Time may not heal all wounds the same way, and you may feel forced to move on or forget about what others have done to you. Keep moving forward and surround yourself with those who have never lost sight of you or questioned who you are for even a second. Your truest thoughts and emotions are repercussions from previous experiences of those who may have abused it. Accept that the past is the past and it could never be your future. Rejoice in the now and the happiness that surrounds you in order to reach a happiness within and nothing truer.

This Beautiful Life

I'm going farther than expected
How beautiful this world is
The best parts in life are those we do not take
for granted
But learn how to see fit

It may be your coffee in the morning
Or even the birds chirping outside
Oh how I will never regret
Living in the moment of this beautiful life

A New World

I don't understand what's occurring
It's like my mind has wandered upon a new place
A place filled with happiness and color
A place where everything comes across much clearer

In this place I am excited
The laughs and smiles become real
The end that I wanted to draw near me
Has become so much further
And all that I thought I had once lost
I am now beginning to feel

Damages

Perhaps time consumed my damage
The tears and unpleasant thoughts
Have nearly come to an end

Whenever I hit a rough patch
I allow my faith to sink in

Life can bloom in even the most damaged spaces
It is up to you on how to take care of it
If you want yours to begin

Reminder:

God prepares moments, sights, and sounds for all
who choose to love him. He has a world full of
color and happiness built just for you. What no
human mind can conceive, He has conjured up for
those who follow him. His scripture is the song
that takes our unsteady souls and calms them. Your
mental state within is what stands apart from you
and the beautiful world our creator has laid out
for you. Go ahead and grab it. Go ahead and take
life full speed ahead and watch God's plan unravel
in your hands. Love the Lord with all of your
heart and allow yourself to dance with him. Allow
yourself to dance with others and never fear to
show people your faith.
Once you learn to spread everlasting love and
happiness through Christ around, you will have
allowed yourself to be beautifully discovered and
found.

How My Mind Operates

I get stuck in these phases where everything is going well for awhile and then in an instant I'm back to feeling emotionless. My anxiety takes over and I have shortness of breath. It takes me a minute to get back to a normal state and gather myself again. I aspire to reach a place where I can sit and feel things like any "normal" person could. A state where I'm alive and no longer have to rely on others' happiness in order to make my own. It's hard being that person that can put on a smile but can't force one when they are alone. Some days are better than others, but nothing is permanent and I slowly lose hope in ever being happy. There comes a time to take action. No matter how bad you want to hurt yourself please don't. It took me time to realize this, but I tucked those feelings away the best I could. I've fallen to my knees plenty of times, begging for an answer as to why these thoughts and feelings had to overcome me every so often. To my amazement, I somehow get up and fall asleep with tears and questions still falling down my face and flooding my mind. But it's the fact that I can get up and still go to bed, even if I'm uneasy that proves there's hope. I know I can't be the only one who feels this way, and I pray for those who haven't found a way to cope or escape. Our minds can be a beautiful thing but can also be the hardest obstacle to deal with day by day. Life is wonderful and magical if you allow it to be, but when someone takes their own it creates a different kind of hurt upon us. Every scar, every dark thought, every bruise you have left on your body... is it really worth it? Mental health is by far one of the most important parts of any human being. We must learn to stand for the lost souls and broken hearts who felt they had no chance of speaking out or healing.

A Good Thing

It never gets easier
Losing someone you once had so much love and lust
for
Reminiscing on every memory you once made
Wishing you were able to make just one more

You stay up thinking about what went wrong
Because deep down in your heart
You thought it was them all along

Now you're both stuck in a trance
Drowning in a pit of denial
Hoping your feelings won't come back at even the
slightest glance of their smile

Knowing damn well you're both suffering from
within
Wishing everything could go back to when you were
just friends

The nights will grow longer and your feelings may
never change
Don't throw away a good thing
Or you will continue to cause each other pain

When You Turn Them Away

Those worth fighting for are often the hardest to
steer away from
You try to deny and forget the memories
But day after day you just become numb

What a mistake it is
To turn down a beautiful soul
Especially One who once made yours blossom so
fully
But the instant you turned them away
Your whole world began to turn ugly

Reminder:

Trying to erase memories from someone who once brought you so much joy can be one of the most painful experiences you may face in life. Constantly being reminded of all the memories that were made but then came to an unsteady halt. You're left feeling you were torn apart from something so good, but you must realize that even sugar looks like salt. I challenge you to not erase these memories but to grow from them. No matter how much we pray for someone to stick around, it won't matter if God doesn't see them in your future. Believe me, this is a hard pill to swallow.

Love suffers long but it is kind. There will be a time where you won't have to remind the right one how to treat you. Continually staying in the Lord's presence will help you see your worth and importance. Don't waste time on things you can't control. When it is sent by God it comes with confirmation and reassurance, but when it isn't sent by God, it comes with hesitation, confusion, jealousy, and anger. Beginnings hide themselves in ends; let this process of change carry you closer to the Lord.

<u>Trapped</u>

Will I make it out of here
This place I've began to call home
Happiness doesn't stay long
But it visits every so often
Once it leaves I'm as lifeless as before
then it props the door open

I hear a whisper behind me
"Welcome home" my mind says
I feel a sense of hopelessness
And find myself gasping for air

Saying nothing at all I slowly get back up
Our silence has a way of translating
Into everything we need to be heard
But not everyone is attuned to hear it

Rest Your Heart

Behind closed doors I am a completely different
person
I crumble and break with even the slightest clue

Not one person would expect it
But no one can hide their pain from <u>You</u>

Struggling to gather myself
I try not to think about anything much more
I know there's a much larger plan for me you have
in store

Learn to Dwell in the land of faithfulness
And rest your heart in the Lord
Despite all things <u>He</u> will save you forevermore

The Effects

When you lay down at night
I hope you sit and reflect
On all of the pain and heartbreak you caused me
I hope you realize all of the effects

But I'll still be here
Living day by day without you knowing
Keeping all of these feelings inside
I can't give off signs of showing

On My Sleeve

What a fool I am
Always putting my heart out on the line for those
who choose to cut it

When will I learn that wearing my heart on my
sleeve
will eventually cause me to plummet

What He Ruins

There are bigger things coming
For This I am sure of
God ruins your plans before your plans ruin you
For this you must make note of

What Comes with Caution

Be cautious of how you treat others
Move in love and not fear

Learn to live with a free mind
And enjoy life with your peers

At times we all get lost
But never leave your heart behind

Those filled with more love then hate
Are often those who have been put through the most
pain

Anxiety

Even on my best days you somehow find me
Causing a tightness in my chest
Breathing becomes harder but I can't resist

Everything happens so fast but feels like it's
lasting forever
Running out of every public place
I just pretend that I'm doing better

Anxiety continually takes control of me
Causing damage in all aspects of my life
Forcing me to turn away from every helping hand
And giving up every single night

I'm holding fast to love and justice
For almost no reason at all

Most of my worst days are conquered with a smile
While I run myself into the ground with ease
Pretending to be happy is what feels comfortable
to me

Reminder:

We all need someone to listen to us. Those who
have always gave me their ears and undivided
attention, I gratefully thank. These are the
people who have openly taken my saddened heart
that continued to break. People that can give us
their own opinion and still help guide us in the
right direction are vital to our growth. We all
have a different story
and with that comes different ways to cope. Being
the person who lends out their attention for those
with no cost are the ones who fill people with a
sense of love and hope.

Although this world is judgemental, there will be
people who generally accept you for who you are
and what your story entails. Believe in starting
over, believe in beginnings after endings, and
believe in humanity. Not everyone is out to get
you and to those who are we need to learn to
forgive. Be the open ear for someone and the voice
that helps them live.

To Be Skinny

You spend most of your nights on the bathroom
floor wishing you could change

It's because I'm bigger isn't it?
Or maybe I'm too small

You don't want me because I have acne on my skin
And you think you have it all

I'm uncomfortable in my own skin 24/7
But I almost never show this

I've been told fat girls need to go to the gym
And the skinny ones need to start eating
But there's so much more to it

Society has a funny way of making us think

That to be skinny you have to starve yourself
To be skinny you have to workout
To be skinny you have to sacrifice everything to
get the person you want
To be skinny you must not care about your overall
health

Behind all of us holds a scary truth
One that we don't want to tell

Consistently judging yourself for not being enough
is hurting you
All to be skinny so you think happiness may come
to you faster

Holding on to the thought of perfection
Your mental health is shattered

Worn

Restless nights keep me feeling empty
Feeling down about things I can't change
I try to focus on a higher power to believe in
I still feel the pain

My heart has been abused
By others and myself

I'm just a worn out human being
Trying to regain its health

The Return of My Diagnosis

When the flashbacks return
Something happens to me

The remembrance of bloodshed
And the scars left behind
will always defy me

Is there any hope left
For what has not yet been taken
My mind and body are in constant recovery
But the fragility of my mind must not be mistaken

With A Person

So many emotions go with one person
And to think we have met so many
There are very few who leave everlasting impacts
Never allowing us to feel at all that empty

To Rewrite Your Life

Look at the fine print of your life
If your thoughts appeared on your skin
How would others interpret you?
Would you reconsider what you think or write?

Wordly expectations drive our energy and happiness
to scatter
Draining your mind, body, and soul
Pieces of you left vulnerable and tattered

The Ugly Truth

We are stuck in our heads

We are filled with constant despair and denial
Going out in public isn't all one may expect
But we hide it behind a smile

Being reminded of all the things on your body that
need repair
Your heart is left wide open
And your mind is filled with fear

This society isn't perfect
And no one should act like it is
Especially when so many are struggling
From very deep within

Submerged

As I submerge myself into a field of dandelions
and daisies
I feel overwhelmed with peace

Feeling the breeze gently glide over my skin
I rewind back to a time where I was happiest

I take a deep breath
I drown out all of the noise inside

Only hearing the sounds of birds chirping
With slight notes of grass swaying in the wind

Life begins to feel balanced
When you learn to control everything within

The Cancer That Took You

Vibrant and outgoing soul
It seemed as though nothing could stop you

From consistent falls and agony placed upon you
To the long nights laying beside you in those
sterilized rooms

You had made it
You seemed to beat what was killing you every time

But the human body can only go on for so long
And what appeared to be healed soon took a turn
for the worst

That treacherous thing began to turn you into
something worse Something less vibrant and less
soulful
You never lost hope, you still have fight left in
you

You have pushed your limits and exceeded
expectations
But it is time to let go and stop all of the
fighting
The thing that took you both is gone
And Heaven is patiently waiting

Finding Happiness

My confidence becomes lost in the mix of emotions,
thoughts, and the occasional bottle of wine
Although this does not help, it sure seemed to at
the time

Drowning my fears and feelings in a drink always
seemed right
But ignoring everything good for me was just me
being stubborn at the time

The difficult times make us stronger
And no matter how much struggle you experience
The Lord will never stop working on you

Happiness can be found and it will if you give it
time
Challenge yourself to learn to walk by Faith,
instead of your sight

Romans 8:18

I'm trying to be the person I needed when I was younger. I find the same type of hurt that I've felt in those who are still young and learning. The thing about pain is that it's a universal feeling. It engulfs us and makes us feel like nothing is working. If you find that you have no one to understand you… let me be the one. Let me show you that pain happens to everyone. I know what it's like to feel hopeless. I know what it's like to have forced pain upon myself because I felt inadequate. Fortunately, I also know what it's like to find hope again. This hope was not easily found, and it took many long nights of questioning and tears in order to get here. Once I began dedicating my life to Christ, things began to fall in place.

Sufferings of this present time are not worth comparing to the glory that is to be revealed to us later. Read this statement over and over again if you have to. If you must sulk, do not let it consume you entirely. Open up to the Lord and use your heart to give others strength and comfort as Christ works His way into your life. When others lose their way, be the one who gives them hope on who God intended them to be. It's a tough world out there, but one day you will look back and thank yourself for never giving up. Those who tend to overthink are also those who over love.

The Emptiness Inside

Pretending is all fun and games until you can't
pretend anymore
The second you become vulnerable everyone notices
Every good thing is engulfed in pain
Every emotion becomes nothing at all
This feeling is almost paralyzing

It's embarrassing to feel this way
It's embarrassing to always have to pretend you're
okay
It's embarrassing to have people come to you for
guidance when you can't find any yourself

You spend your time worrying over and over
Constantly putting yourself down
Regretting why you ever tried to be happy knowing
damn well you aren't

You've created a false hope in yourself
You've successfully tricked your mind into
believing something you're not

Congratulations... have fun trying to sleep this
one off

Recovery

So badly I want you to understand

I want you to understand that this isn't easy for me
I want you to understand that there are days I don't feel alive
I want you to understand that I just need to be alone sometimes

But I also want you to understand that I am trying
Every day is different and comes with multiple challenges
Try to understand and please bear with me
It's a very long process
This thing we call recovery

Reminder

There are going to be days where nothing seems right. On these days you feel alone and like the world is against you. You are right about one thing... the world is against you. In fact, the world would love nothing more than to claim you as its own. Little do you know, the Lord chose you to come out of the world, and that's why it feels like everything is crashing down around you. Finding happiness in worldly things will blind your way into finding happiness through the Lord. You have the love of Jesus in you. Let me remind you that you are not alone and you were hand picked by God to do more than just sit on your bathroom floor and sulk. As long as we remain in Him, He will remain in us. Rejoicing in our suffering produces endurance, character, and hope.

The Cost

Learn to love and give back no matter the cost
At times people will hate you because of the way
others love you

But with high hopes we are filled with enough
strength to make it through

One day all of the love that you have given away
so selflessly will come back to you

God only knows what you've been through
Don't be ashamed or afraid

What is consistently taken for granted
Is eventually taken away

Purity

My longing soul is surrounded by the sounds of
rain and sweet melancholies

Abiding in nothing but my own sadness
An overflow of joyousness comes upon me

Purify me Lord
Purify me of these demeaning and nasty thoughts
Purify me of the worldly things I have let take
control
Purify me in this very spot

It Is Kind

Rejoicing in our sufferings is like learning how
to breathe again

There's no tightness or insecurity
Nothing binding you inside

It's finally feeling peace within
Living a fulfilled life once again
Love may suffer long
But it is kind in the end

Self-Concept

The way we view ourselves is a reflection of how
the most important people in our lives view us

But when we are surrounded by love and good people
yet still feel sad, there's something that's not
adding up

Our hearts long for God's glory
Yet the fear of rejection has led us to
manipulation

Stop looking to be apart of a solution
And let God use you in any given situation

Growth

Peace grows abundantly in the minds and souls of
those who choose to let grace lead them

With fields of wildflowers covering their path
No evil will be allowed to sneak in

Learn to live in your true center
So the power of love may strengthen your heart

Happiness will soon take over your weaknesses
Each day is left feeling like a brand-new start

A Woman

If you are trying to be like Jesus
Be the one who never gives up on others
Showing grace and forgiveness even when everyone
leaves

This is the woman I have aimed to be

A woman who makes mistakes
But knows the importance of repentance

A woman who has a true heart filled with faith and
love
And knows how to give it

I've made many strides and I still stick with Him
For by the grace of God I am able to be His child
Indeed, the definition of a strong and lovable
woman

Our Calling

I hope you find your happiness
Even if it's not within me

If now isn't the time
Maybe one day it will be

So that all the love we have given out
Will come back to us in full swing

Refreshed

As the smell of freshly bloomed lilacs gather my
attention
I am quickly reminded of the purity this world may
hold

Inhaling and exhaling a little deeper
I begin to get lost in a panorama of untouched
beauty
A view that will never get old

Anxiety

When my heart experiences a sudden falling
And a numbness takes over my body

Everything soon becomes weak
My mind becomes a terrible place to reside, yet I
have no idea what's happening me

The feeling of 10,000 pounds crushing my chest
restricts me from any sudden movement

Despite the constant laughter and boisterous
outbreaks in my tone
I am suffering from something that is extremely
well-known

It is known as Anxiety to many
But to me it's my truth

With a fear of never being enough
My mind quickly becomes unglued

What Comes With Age

As we age
Everything we once made a big deal
Now means little to nothing

The small and large fights made us stronger
The little things are what matter most
Just the smell of coffee makes you feel more awake

We realize that our parents were stern to teach us
a lesson
And it's okay to give and receive discipline

No one is perfect, and with age we are shown this
The world isn't always blissful
But we make the most of it

Limitless

For years I held a grudge against you for the way
you treated others
The way you treated me

Today I realized how much harder that has been on
me than on you
And how you've changed tremendously

Although we may have our reasons, who are we not
to forgive others?

Extend unlimited forgiveness
Keep your heart open and pure

The world and its nonstop demands can be put on
hold
Take a deep breath and learn to let things go

Reminder

The cultivation of love becomes present to us when
we allow ourselves to be vulnerable. We fall in
love with potential but never allow ourselves to
go for it fully. Just because some of us carry it
so well does not mean it isn't heavy.
Our Lord not only drives us to be authentic, but
He does not allow us to be what we are not.
Concentrate on staying close to your faith even
when your fears and anxieties take over your
thoughts. When we are willing to show others our
weaknesses we become much stronger. How close we
are to the Lord may determine His willingness to
bless others around us. Bits and pieces of heaven
are hidden in our hearts and we can call on them
in every moment of our day. Let the light shine
upon you and you will be saved.

Where You Are Now

Vivacious wanderer
Oh how far you've come

From sleepless nights
To days you wanted to quickly end

You became a carefree walk to the creek
You finally became your own friend

It's in your eyes now
True happiness and grace

Letting the little things go
Putting behind all of your pain

I'm Still Broken

The tug in my chest is unexplainable
I begin to form tears in the creases of my eyes
I thought I was fixed
I thought I was finding my own light

I'm caught staring at the ground
Thinking about my damaged parts

Too afraid to show it
I quickly reassure myself that I'm happy

I'm happy right?
Please someone convince me that I am

With a fear of repressing
It's to my own mind that I give in

Thoughts of death cross my mind
But I don't have the strength to do this

There's a life out there worth living
I just need to pursue it

With Faith

The amount of courage I have to muster up is
unbearable when I want to make an appearance

But I must not be ashamed of my emptiness
I must not allow others to see it

They don't know how bad I'm broken
Masking the severity of my depression seems easy
in the moment
As soon as I return home I can't control this

Slamming my steering wheel as I drive
I rest on the side of a gravel road where I take a
deep breath
I'm beginning to feel lost and unsteady
My breathing becomes fast paced, short, and heavy

Cursing aloud I question why I am tossed in these
emotions
I think about my siblings
I think about my godson, my cousins
I think about how far my family has come
And I think about the ones lost because of this

My purpose may not be clear just yet
My emotions may not always be stable
But my heart holds the hope of Heaven in it
With Faith I am capable

Invisibility

The poison to our soul is derived from bitterness,
jealousy, hostility, and judgement

We may sound confident
Yet, have anxiety
We may appear happy on the outside
Yet, inside we feel defeated

Maybe you're not healing because you wish to go
back to the person you were before you felt all of
this pain
Maybe you're healing by scabs forming over your
cuts

Mental illness is invisible
Yet, it so clearly affects many of us

Sadness

The kind of sorrow God wants us to experience
leads us away from sin
The kind of sorrow that's so true that it leads us
to joy

The more we humble ourselves and admit to our
weaknesses
The more joy we are able to experience

For He gives us what He knows we can handle
And surrounds us in the hope that is forever alive

To feel sorrow means we are able to feel happy
again
Those tears you so often shed, will begin to dry

Soulmate

As the feeling of wasted time is continued
I am pressured to speak up

Feeling like I should say something but am
silenced by the fact that I never feel good enough

No wonder you show no interest in me
Now wonder you could care less about how I was
doing

Although it hurts now, it's a place I ache to go
back to again
A place where I felt someone cared about me for
once, loved me for who I am

But I am not like most
I do not give into worldly things or sexual
intentions easily

I take pride in staying faithful
I take pride in getting to know someone before I
rush in

I pray the day I find my soulmate I feel
completely at peace
For now I wait and continue to pray
Even though each trial is left in utter disbelief

What We Choose

In the end I hope you choose life
I hope you give out everlasting forgiveness
And I hope you allow your heart to break and turn
it into lessons

Misunderstandings may disrupt your daily life no
matter your good intentions
And pure motives are not always viewed how you'd
like to believe they are no matter your situation

Many of us are angry, empty, and lost
But each of us deserve to feel whole again

Learn the value of patience, vulnerability, and
looking past worthless things
Realize peace is achievable
It's not just an elusive goal in the end

The Trials of Today

As the shimmering sunshine awakens your soul
You are reminded of the beauty of life

Be thankful for quiet days
Be thankful for sadness
Be thankful that once you were lost
Someone wanted to help you find happiness

The best way to handle unwanted situations
Is to thank the Lord for them

Submerge yourself in the trials of today
Take pride in what you may accomplish tomorrow
Nothing is unachievable
When you live a life full of Christ instead of
sorrow

Reminder

As we grow older, we learn to not take everything as seriously as before. All of the lectures, the occasional fights with our parents, and the people that used to talk down on us, are all lessons learned. At the end of the day, I'm thankful for my struggles. I'm thankful for my parents being strict, and I'm thankful for having to work for everything that I have. These things have all impacted me differently, both negatively and positively, but have shaped me into who I am. I was never the perfect daughter, friend, or the right spouse for some, and never will be. It's the fact that I continue to strive to be the best version of myself that allows me to keep building.

Where I Am

I'm gone
But I'm better off here for I cannot be tied down

Living each day with no plan in store
Taking in the life ahead of me
My mind begins to wander

I belong in a world full of never-ending
possibilities
Feeling the breeze gently glide through my hair
and on top of my skin
What a world this is
I take another deep breath in

I'm sincere, courageous, and full of life
A full-blown wild child
With a creative mind

The gray areas that once covered my sky
Have now been covered in color and replaced with a
different kind

My story. My Conclusion.

For years I hid most of the damage I had done to myself behind closed doors. Not wanting even my parents to know what I've done to myself, I only continued to do it more.

From nights where I would pray to never wake up, I regret now those thoughts and derogatory statements I'd convinced myself were true.

Unfortunately, this is not something easy for me to admit, but being vulnerable is okay. I am okay. And this is my truth.

From making slight incisions into my skin, to carving words into areas of my stomach, I was normally left feeling defeated. I've learned that having scars only means those areas have healed over. If my skin can do it, so can I. That was the only proof that I needed.

How lost I once was only brought fear of the possibility of these thoughts returning. Putting myself in a constant anxious state, I would continually break out in sudden attacks throughout the day. I was embarrassed and terrified at the things that would run through my head during this time. I felt like my mental health needed to be hidden as I put on a front of being happy and confident. To others this was the Morgan they knew, but most of the time it was all a lie. In the last year I have had the opportunity to recover and finally seek the help that I owe to myself. Writing this book has taught me one thing, and that is I am far too young to say goodbye.

With millions of other people dealing with what I do and worse, mental health goes far beyond my story. I encourage you to be vulnerable and seek help. Tell your parents and your friends how you feel. It took me years to tell mine what I put myself through, but when I did, I felt a weight lifted off my shoulders and knew I had never been alone this whole time.

My name is Morgan Mortimer, and I'm insecure about my body, I get anxiety often, I feel like I am not good enough for anyone, and I have scars on my body that I don't want anyone to see.

I have learned that being vulnerable is not a bad thing, and I'm not afraid to share my story anymore.

My name is Morgan Mortimer and I know that I put forth so much effort toward everything that I do, love much harder than I should, and fall in love just the same. I am smart, and I'm willing to do whatever I have to do to get to where I want to be, and if you don't like me that's okay.

It's about time we start opening up and allow ourselves to be vulnerable every once in a while. **It's okay to be genuine and kind to those that may not deserve it, and it's okay to be genuine and kind to yourself**. This is **What Lead Us to New Beginnings**, and this is my story.

The End.

Special thanks to all of my family, friends, and those who have stuck by my side through this entire journey. No process of this project was easy but would have never been attainable without them. Also, special thanks to Jeremy Rehwaldt who not only gave me advice but went through each poem and made the correct changes necessary to make everything flow together. I will be forever grateful.

With many thanks and blessings,
Morgan Mortimer

About The Author

Morgan Mortimer has always been known to go above and beyond on any project or obstacle thrown her way. As a young aspiring author/designer who felt barricaded by her small town, it was time for her to fully break out of her shell and discover who she really wanted to be. The transition from corn fields and cattle to paved streets and stoplights was only the beginning of a new world and opportunities for this hometown girl. Morgan's projects are meant to bring out emotions people experience all throughout life and relate to those who have felt silenced. She aims to spread light on arising social issues and be a helping hand for those in need.